WARNING!

Lots of crazy words!

i

Author: Matthew Hitch

Co-author: Sunok Moon

Illustrator: Matthew Hitch

Cover Design: Brittany Hitch

Layout Design: Matthew Hitch

Text Design: Matthew Hitch

Image Manager: Matthew Hitch

~~Vain Meglomaniac: Matthew Hitch~~

Credits Editor: Matthew Hitch

Image Manager Manager: S. Moon

Image Manager Manager Control: Absolutely no one

Artistic Arguer: Sunok Moon

Dishwasher: Matthew Hitch
(occasionally Sunok Moon)

Title: Captain Matt's Super Crazy Fun

Preschool Phonics 2   Student Book

ISBN 979-11-982546-6-5

First published 2023

Published by Hitch Publishing

info@supercrazyfun.net

This textbook came about as the result of 20 years of trying to make kids enjoy learning English. It is designed around the use of the rhotic R and other characteristics of English pronunciation common in North America. We believe it can be used in other parts of the world as most phonics books can, and we are keen to hear feedback from anyone who tries this.

We want to make clear that the word "crazy" used in the title is in relation to any of the common definitions illustrated below, and does not refer in any way to the meaning "insane."

strange/illogical   **wild**   **unexpected**   **fun**   **unwise**

About the Authors:

Matthew Hitch has taught English in Korea for the better part of 20 years and holds a master's degree in applied linguistics. He clearly does not have a pig nose, and by most accounts is not at all malodorous. He also cuts a dashing figure according to his wife.

Sunok Moon prefers to go by the name Michelle, and is in fact quite scary as reported in the bio on the back of this book. She has a degree in English literature and has taught English in Korea for approximately 3 weeks longer than Matthew, who is writing this and finds it weird to refer to himself in the third person.

Contents

Welcome parents and teachers!

Thank you for considering our book. Phonics books are notoriously boring, so this is the last bastion of publishing where even the tiniest bit of creativity can raise the bar (sorry phonics book publishers, but it's true). With that said, we humbly offer you our content. We have also intentionally challenged convention in a few ways. Much of what we have to say may be used or discarded though, and these books can be used just like any other mainstream phonics book. We hope you will choose to use whatever you please and dispose of the rest.

Please allow us to explain just where our method of teaching phonics may diverge from mainstream approaches, and please do forgive us for sharing information from what is undeniably the most mind-numbingly boring and seemingly useless field of study, linguistics. Most phonics books are not written by scholars in the field of linguistics. They are mostly written by early childhood educators, so perhaps that's the first divergence. We'll start with how we sound out consonants. In linguistic studies it is not uncommon for consonants to be distinguished by using a vowel (usually "ah") on both sides. This means a "V" sounds like "ahvah" and an "F" sounds like "ahfah" and so on. Most phonics books distinguish consonant sounds without such preceding vowel, but they do follow with a vowel in the form of the schwa. This is fine for most consonants, but the ones that are able to be maintained until breath is exhausted can be confusing with a schwa where they end a word. It's mostly ESL students who feel this confusion, but we think it doesn't hurt to teach those consonants without a schwa to native speakers as well, so where "V" sounds like "və" in most phonics books, in our book it is presented as "vvvvvvv" with no schwa. We apply this to all long consonant sounds in our audio files (L,M,N&R are also presented as long with a tiny schwa sound at the end though). If you have read this far, we take our hats off to you. Most would be fast asleep by now.

The next divergence is our use of Magic E. We chose Magic E for the fun potential. The Split Digraphs just can't seem to hold a crowd. Magic E is no longer used in most educational settings for many reasons, but mostly because as a rule it cannot be defined clearly. We do mention that split digraphs are better though, mainly to extend an olive branch to all the teachers we hope will buy our books.

And the final divergence we would like to mention is our choice of words. Our choice of words may seem a bit odd at times throughout the books, but we chose them for their potential for keeping kids engaged over their usefulness. We approach a phonics book as a tool to teach about sounds much more than vocabulary. Poop, vomit, spit, fart, snot, and burp are the most popular with our students. We tried to find a spot for booger, but alas...

Our word choice is also strange in that it includes words that have the long E vowel when teaching split digraphs. Most phonics books glance over the long E vowel. The argument we have heard for this is that it is difficult for the younger students, but we suspect that it's avoided more because it's difficult for authors to find suitable words. We decided to give it a try, and our experience is that the long E words we chose are not that difficult for our students to grasp. Given that English is their second language, we believe native English speaking kids will cope with them just fine. Also you may notice our sight words are not all actually sight words - oops! Anyway, we hope you enjoy our silly books.

Welcome students!

Okay, so now let's learn
how to put sounds together.

Tracks 0-9

We write them close together,
so we say them close together!

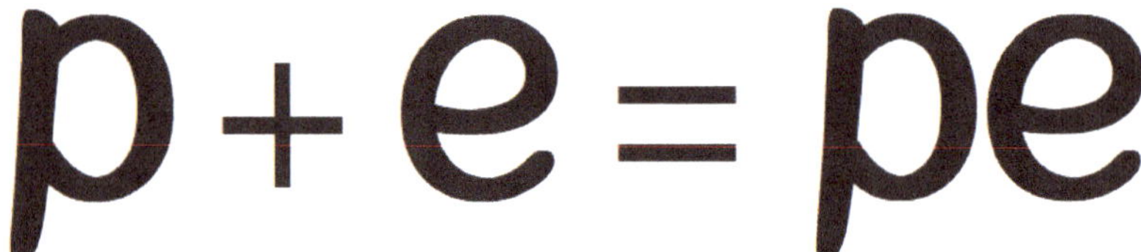

$$p + e = pe$$

But we don't just write them close together like a bunch of grapes!

They all have to be in a straight line!

Let's get started...

Sounds

Vowels

Tracks 0-9

Name	Sound
A	a
E	e
I	i
O	o
U	u

The name is long. The sound is short. i and u can sound VERY short!

Vowels are a bit like glue sticking other letters together to make words!

6   Sounds

"Sometimes Sounds"

Many letters have a "sometimes sound."
Sometimes the letter A makes the same
sound as the letter U!
You can hear it in the word "banana."
We use that sometimes sound for the word "a."

Tracks 0-9

Track 7

Practice with your teacher:

Track 8

1.	2.	3.	4.
	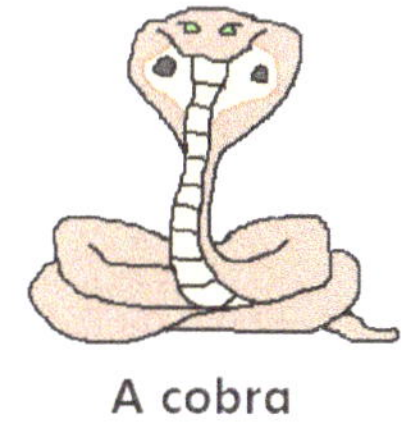		
A banana	A cobra	A pizza	A panda

UNIT 1   Short Vowel Sounds

Listen, point, and make the sound:   Words with a 

Tracks 0-9

1   a + m = am

2   a + g = ag

3   a + d = ad

Listen, point, and say the word: 

1   h + am = ham      ham

2   b + ag = bag      bag

3   d + ad = dad      dad

Follow the rules

Write the words

1 h + am = _______________ 

2 b + ag = _______________ 

3 d + ad = _______________ 

4 m + an = _______________ 

New Words

Tracks 10-19

ad

bad   **dad**

ag

bag   **nag**

am

ham   **jam**

an

fan   **man**

ap

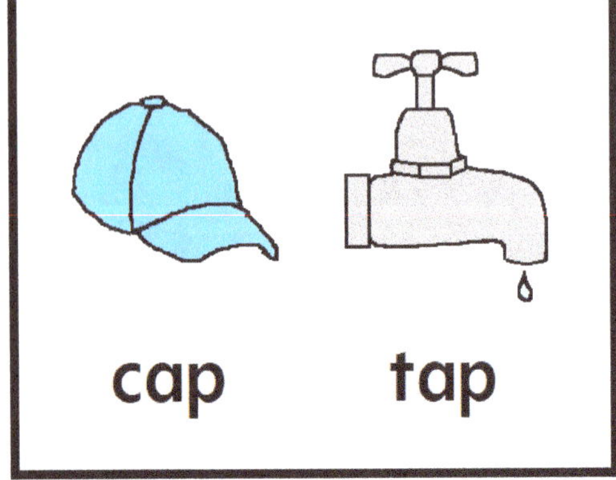

cap   **tap**

at

fat   **rat**

Exercises

Listen and write the last two letters

Tracks 10-19

1  j ________

2 n ________

3 b ____________

4 f ____________

Listen and circle the right letters AND picture

1 am ap ad 

2 am ag an 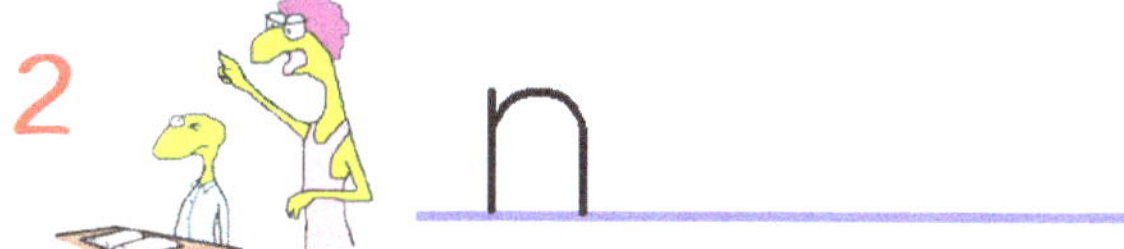

3 ap ag ad 

4 an at ap 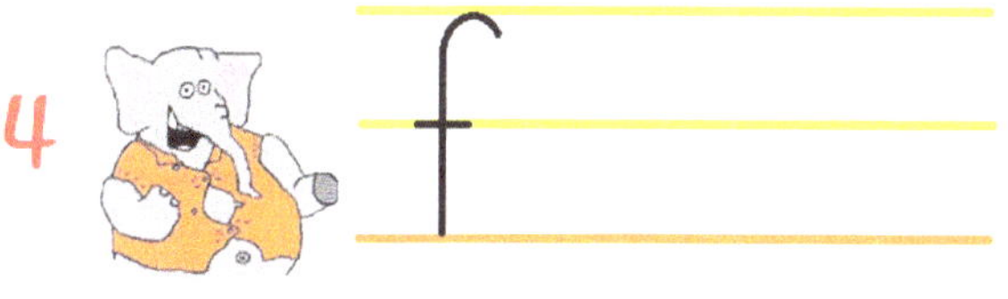

5 ap ag at 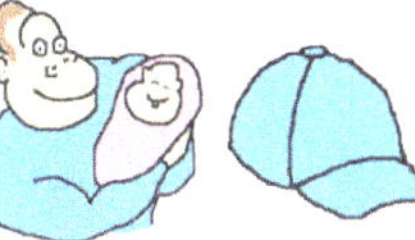  

6 am ag ad  

Exercises

Circle the word you hear

Tracks 10-19

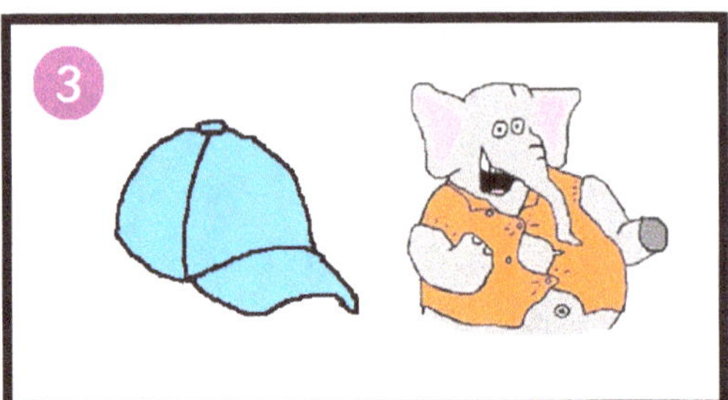

Write the word to match the picture

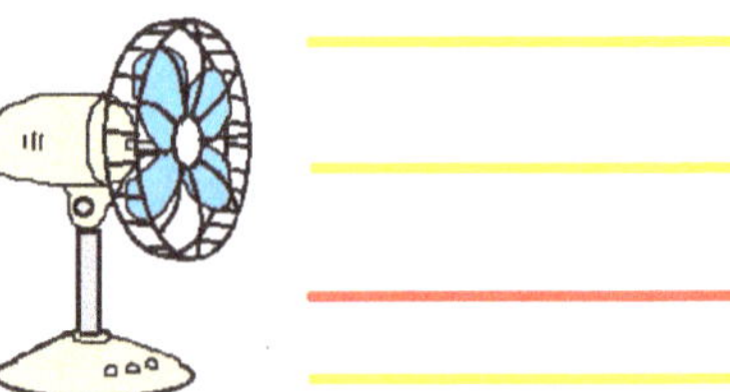

Chant

Nag the man,

nag the man,

nag the bad man.

Turn off the tap!

Turn off the fan!

Story

Circle the last two letters of the word you hear

Tracks 10-19

1. am ag ad   2. am ap at

3. an at ad   4. am ag an

Listen and read along

New sight words: my   am

UNIT 2   Short Vowel Sounds

Listen, point, and make the sound:  Track 18 Words with e 

1   e + n = en

2   e + d = ed

3   e + g = eg

Listen, point, and say the word: Track 19

1   m + en = men  men

2   r + ed = red 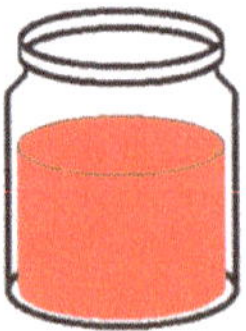 red

3   l + eg = leg 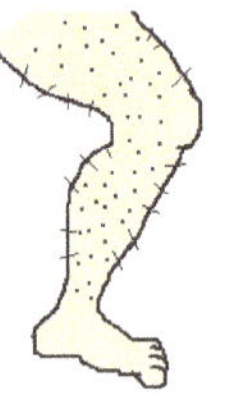 leg

Follow the rules

1 m + en = __________ 

2 r + ed = __________ 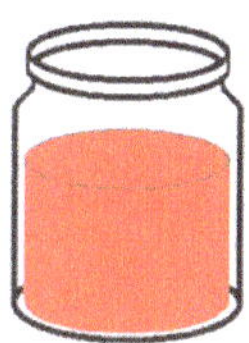

3 l + eg = __________ 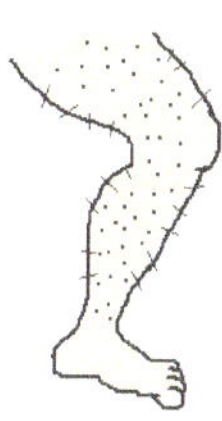

4 w + et = __________ 

New Words

Track 20

Tracks 20-29

eb

Deb   **web**

ed

red   **wed**

eg

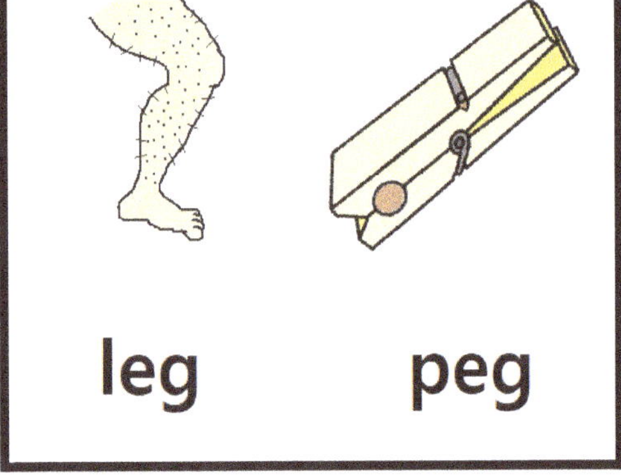

leg   **peg**

ell

bell   **well**

en

men   **pen**

et

pet   **wet**

Exercises

Listen and write the last two letters

Tracks 20-29

1 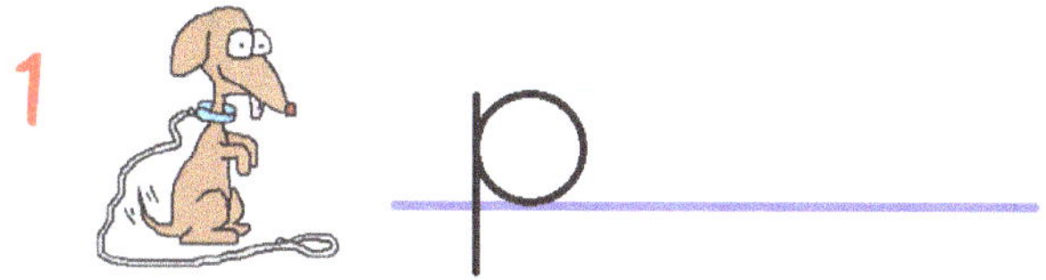 p ___________

2 p ___________

3 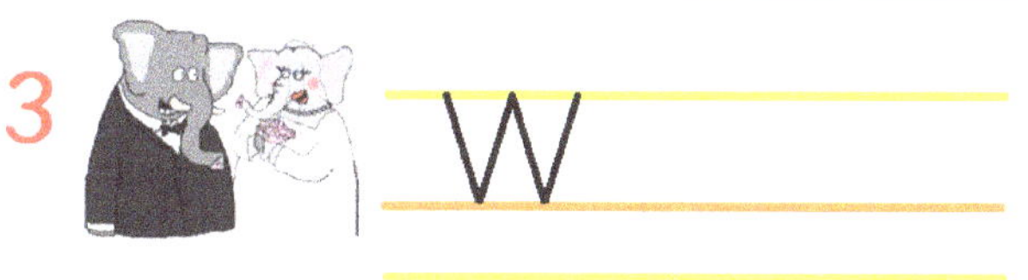 W ___________

4  W ___________

Listen and circle the right letters AND picture

1 en ell eg 

2 et ed eb 

3 en ell ed 

4 et eb eg 

5 eg en ed 

6 ell et eb 

Exercises

Circle the word you hear

Tracks 20-29

Write the word to match the picture

Chant

New sight words: she   wear   so

Peg Leg Deb,

She wears red,

So, so scary,

Peg Leg Deb.

18   Unit 2

Story

Circle the last two letters of the word you hear

Track 25

Tracks 20-25

1. ed   eb   eg
2. ed   eb   ell
3. en   ell   et
4. et   en   ell

Listen and read along

Track 26

New sight words: will

UNIT 3   Short Vowel Sounds

Listen, point, and make the sound:   Track 27 Words with i 

Tracks 20-29

1   i + n = in

2   i + p = ip

3   i + g = ig

Listen, point, and say the word: Track 28 

1 b + in = bin   bin

2 r + ip = rip   rip

3 w + ig = wig    wig

Follow the rules

Write the words

1 b + in = ___________ 

2 r + ig = ___________ 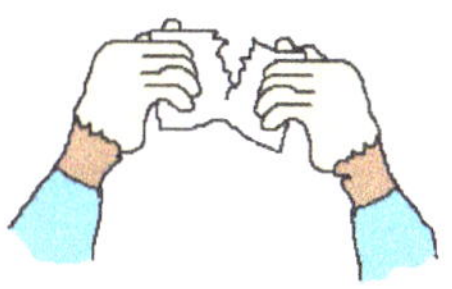

3 w + ig = ___________ 

4 + it = ___________ 

New Words

Listen, point and repeat the new words

Track 29

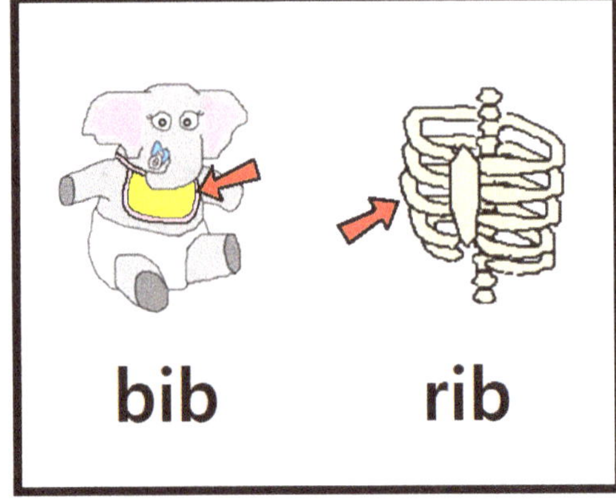

ib bib rib

id kid lid

ig big wig

in bin fin

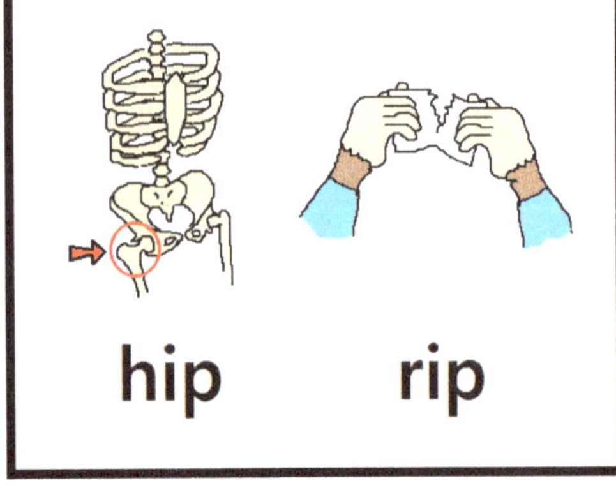

ip hip rip

it hit sit

Exercises

Listen and write the last two letters 

Tracks 30-39

1 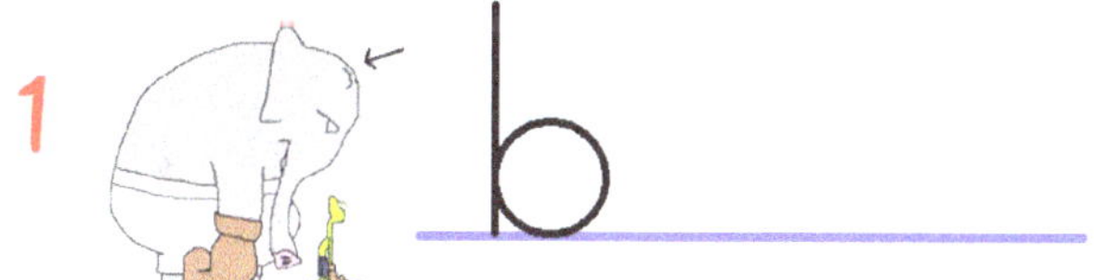 b ____________

2 h ____________

3 f ____________

4 h ____________

Listen and circle the right letters AND picture

1 ib ip in 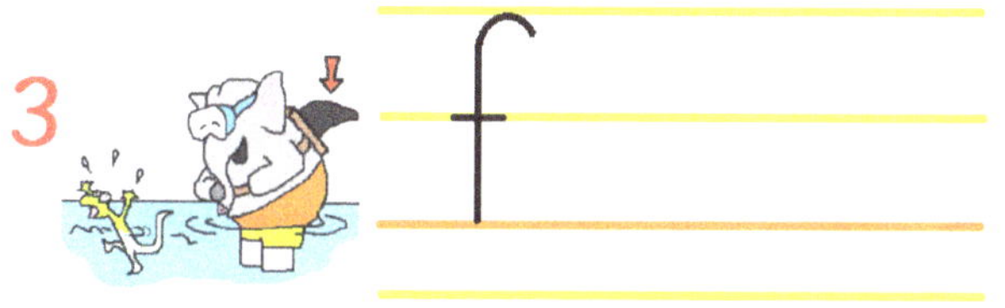

2 id in ib 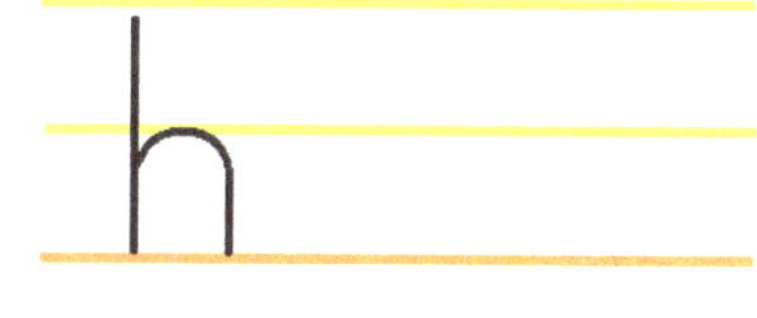

3 ip it ig 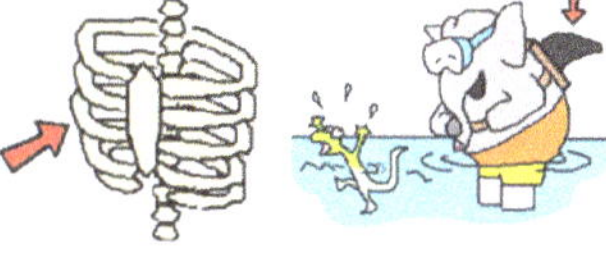

4 id ib it 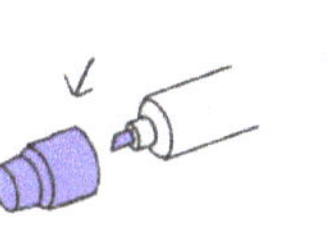

5 id ig it 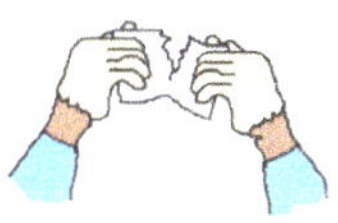

6 ip in ig 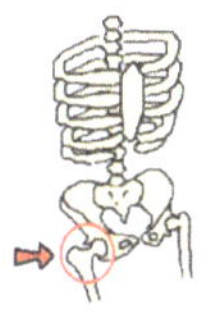

Exercises

Circle the word you hear

Track 32

Tracks 30-39

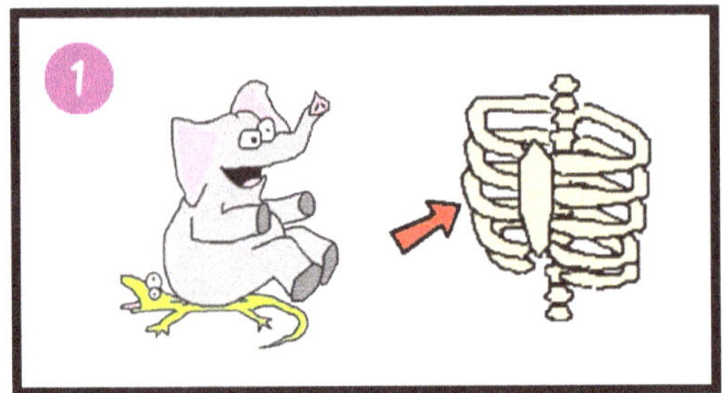

Write the word to match the picture

 __________________

New sight words: want   give   me

Chant

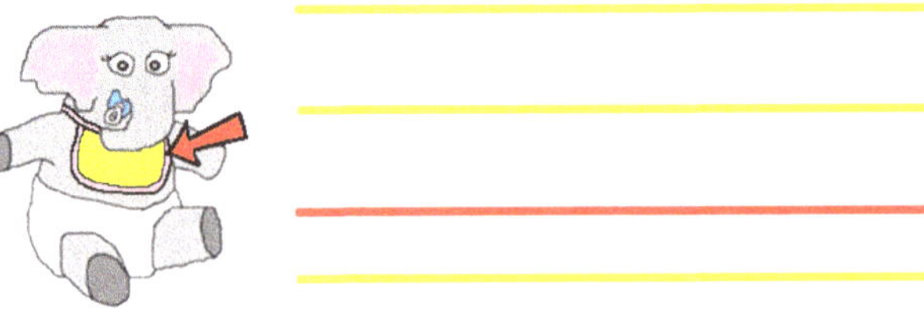

Big kid sits in a bib.
Big kid sits in a bib.

I want ribs!
Give me ribs!

Big kid sits in a bib.

Track 33

Story

Circle the last two letters of the word you hear

Tracks 30-39

1 ib ig ip   **2** ib ig ip

3 it id in   **4** it id in

Listen and read along

New sight words: have

I am Fin Man!

I have a big fin!

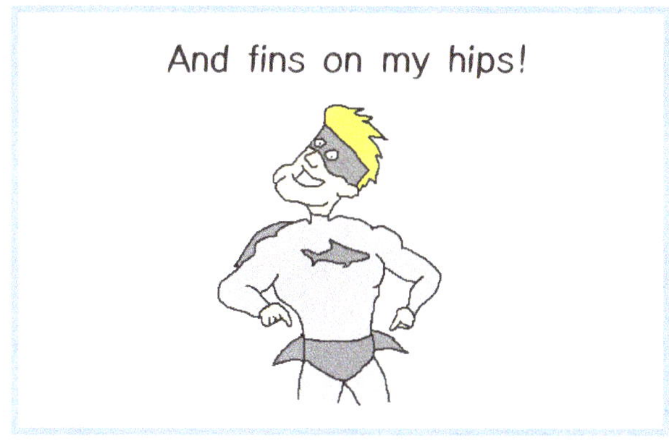
And fins on my hips!

And I wear a wig...

Review

Tracks 30-39

Track 36

1
ad
ag
am

2
an
ap
at

3
eb
ed
eg

4
ell
en
et

5
ib
id
ig

6
in
ip
it

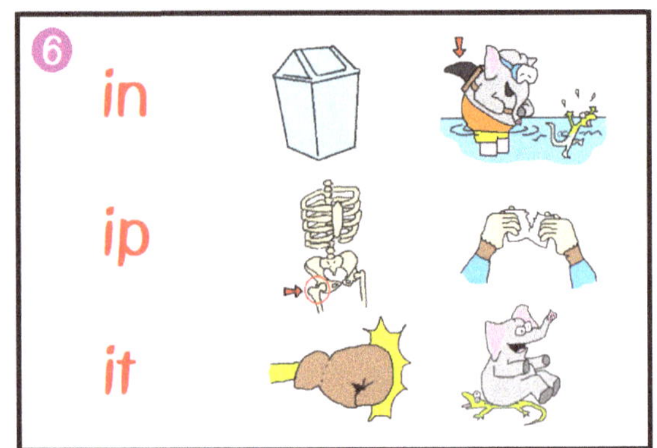

Review

1  _______________

2 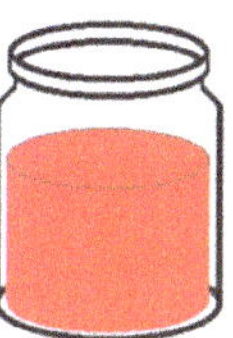 _______________

3  _______________

4  _______________

5  _______________

6 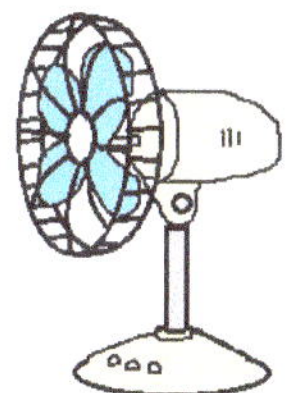 _______________

Review

Find the path

Listen to the final sound and circle the right one

Tracks 30-39

Track 37

1   	2  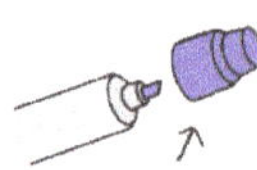 
3  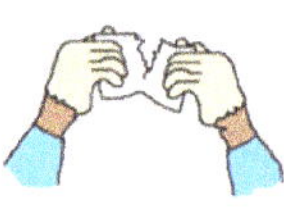 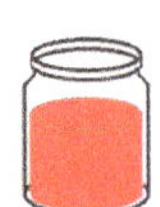	4   

Review  

Listen and circle. Then write the word.

1   _______________________________

2   _______________________________

3 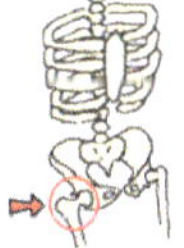  _______________________________

4 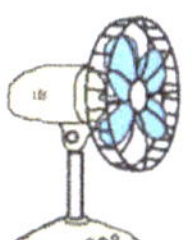  _______________________________

5   _______________________________

Listen, point, and make the sound:   Track 39 Words with o 

Tracks 30-39

1   o + b = ob

2   o + t = ot

3   o + = o

Listen, point, and say the word: Track 40

1   r + ob = rob  rob

2   p + ot = pot 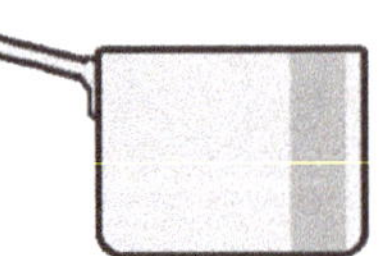 pot

3   b + o = bo 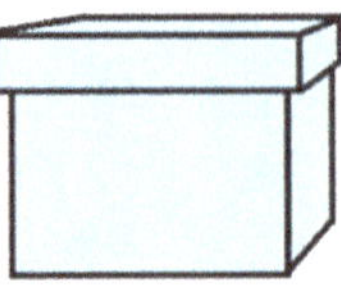 box

Follow the rules

Write the words

1 r + ob = __________ 

2 p + ot = __________ 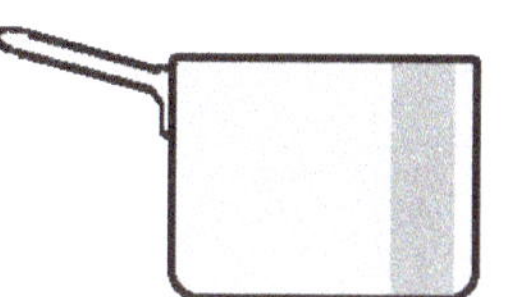

3 b + o = __________

4 d + og = __________ 

New Words

Listen, point and repeat the new words 

ob

rob   **sob**

og

dog   log

on

on   **Ron**

op

hop   mop

ot

got   **pot**

ox

box   **fox**

Exercises

Listen and write the last two letters  

1 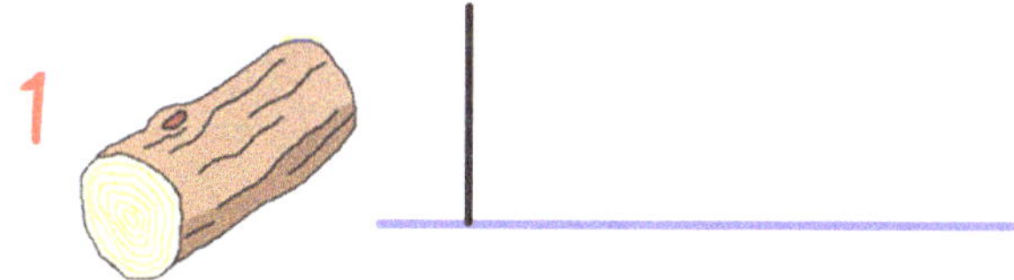 l

2 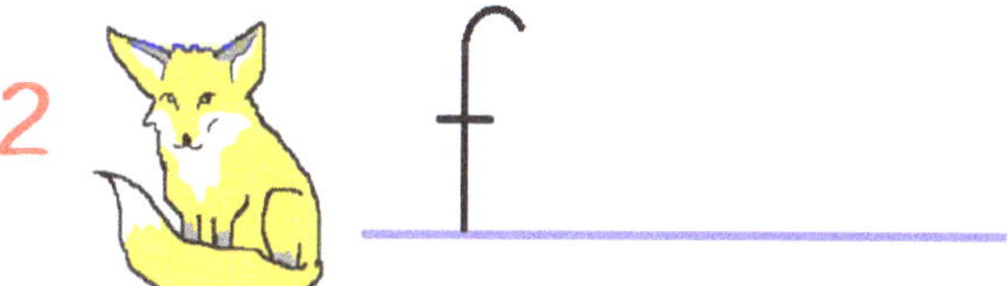 f

3 s

4 m

Listen and circle the right letters AND picture 

1 ot ob on  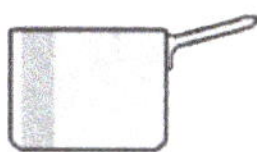

2 og op ox 

3 ob on ot  

4 ox og op 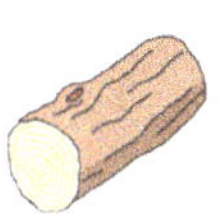 

5 on ot ob  

6 og op ox  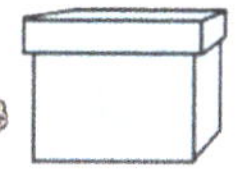

Exercises

Circle the word you hear

Tracks 40-49

Write the word to match the picture

Chant

Dog on a log,
Dog on a log,
He's a handsome
Dog on a log.

Fox in a box,
Fox in a box,
She's a pretty
Fox in a box.

New sight words: he   handsome   pretty

Story

Circle the last two letters of the word you hear

Track 46

Tracks 40-49

1 ot   ob   on   **2** ox   og   op

3 og   op   ox   **4** on   ot   ob

Listen and read along

Track 47

New sight words: Let's what cent

Listen, point, and make the sound:   Track 48 Words with u 

Tracks 40-49

1   u + b = ub

2   u + n = un

3   u + t = ut

Listen, point, and say the word: Track 49

1   t + ub = tub 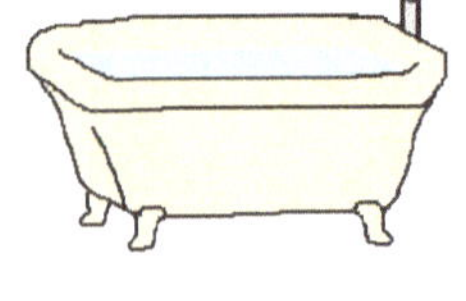 tub

2   f + un = fun 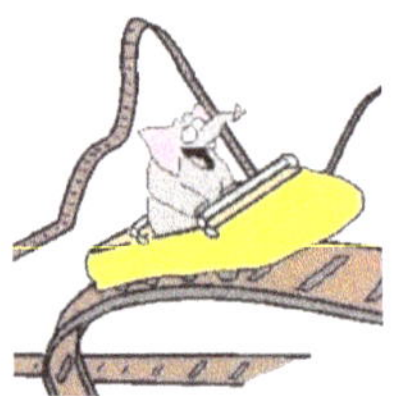 fun

3   h + ut = hut 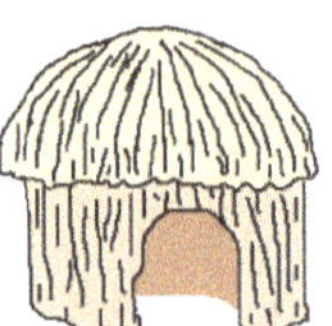 hut

Follow the rules 

Write the words

1. t + ub = ___________ 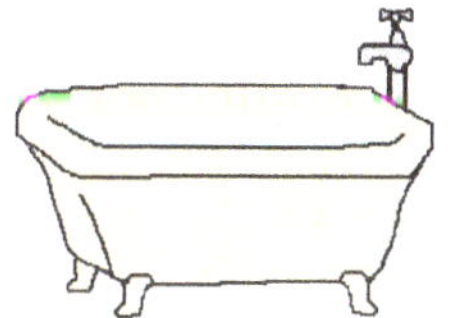

2. + un = ___________ 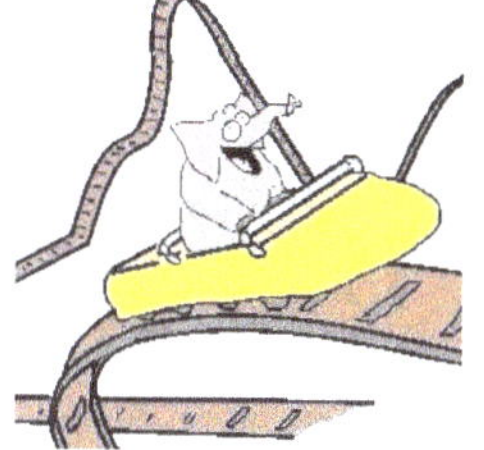

3. + ut = ___________ 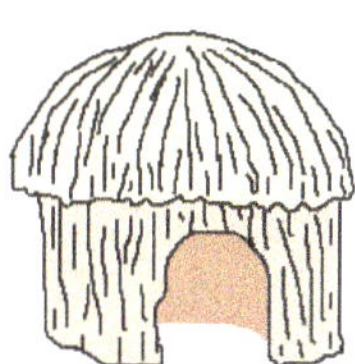

4. m + ud = ___________ 

New Words

Listen, point and repeat the new words

Tracks 50-59

ub 

sub   **tub**

ud 

bud   **mud**

ug 

bug   **hug**

un 

fun   **run**

up 

cup   **pup**

ut 

cut   **hut**

Exercises

Listen and write the last two letters

1  c ______

2 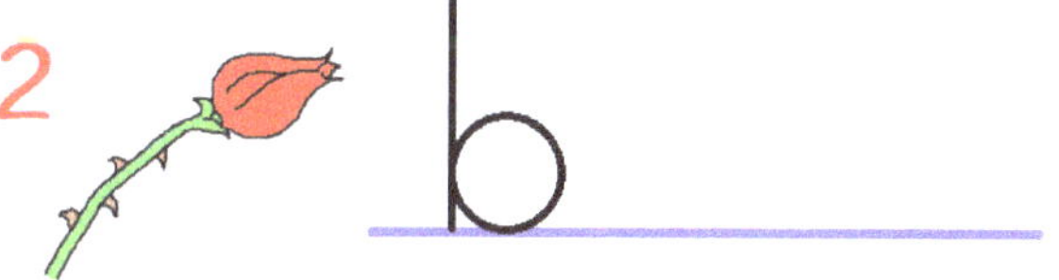 b ______

3 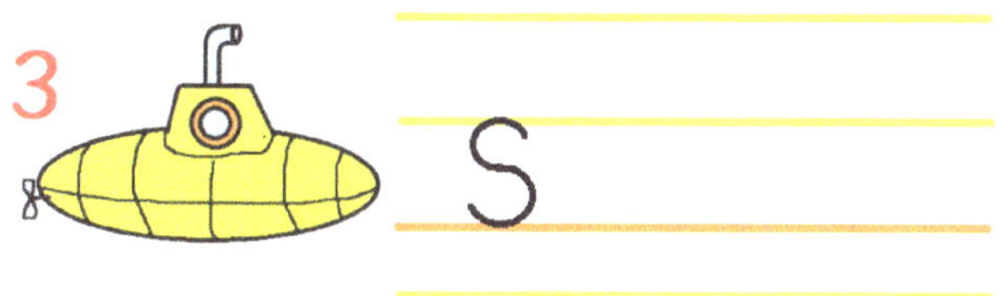 s ______

4 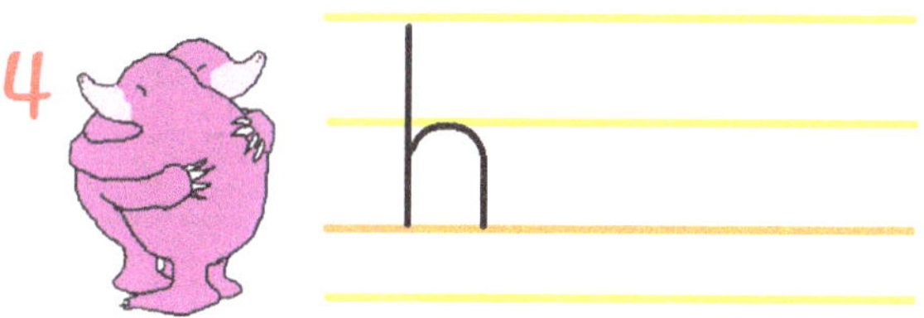 h ______

Listen and circle the right letters AND picture

1 up ug un 

2 ub up ug 

3 ub un ud 

4 ub ug ut 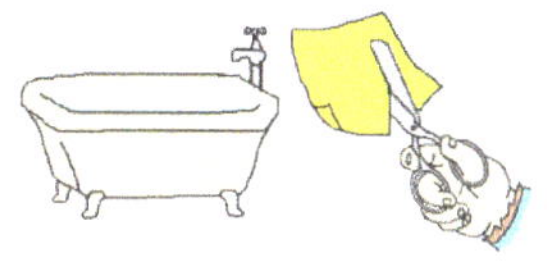

5 up ut ug 

6 ub ud un 

Exercises

Circle the word you hear

Tracks 50-59

Write the word to match the picture

Chant

Run pup,
Run pup run.
Run in the mud,
It's fun fun fun.

Run pup,
Run pup run.
Jump in the tub,
It's fun fun fun.

Story

Circle the last two letters of the word you hear

1. ut   un   up   2. ut   un   up

3. ud   ub   ug   4. ud   ut   ub

Listen and read along

New sight words: see

UNIT 6   Short Vowel Sounds

Listen, point, and make the sound:  Track 57 Words with a, e, i, o, u

Tracks 50-59

1 a + p = ap

2 e + t = et

3 u + s = us

Listen, point, and say the word: Track 58

1 m + ap = map

 map

2 n + et = net

net

3 b + us = bus

bus

Follow the rules 

Write the words

1. m + ap = __________ 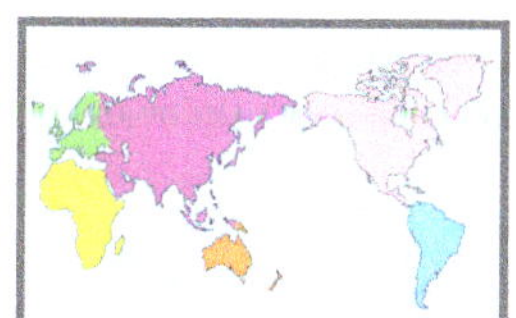

2. n + et = __________ 

3. b + u_ = __________ 

4. c + op = __________ 

New Words

Listen, point and repeat the new words

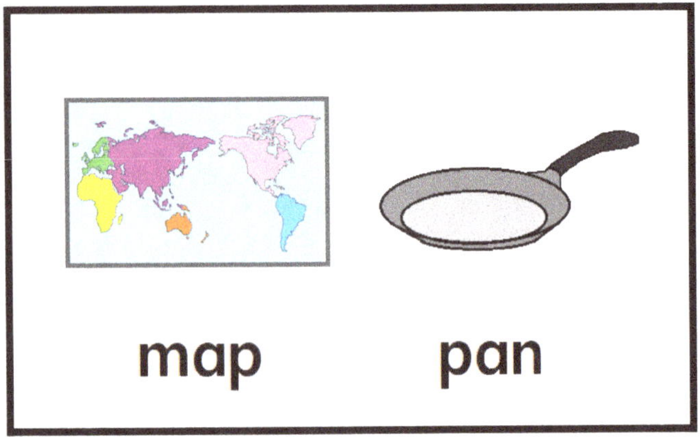

map   **pan**

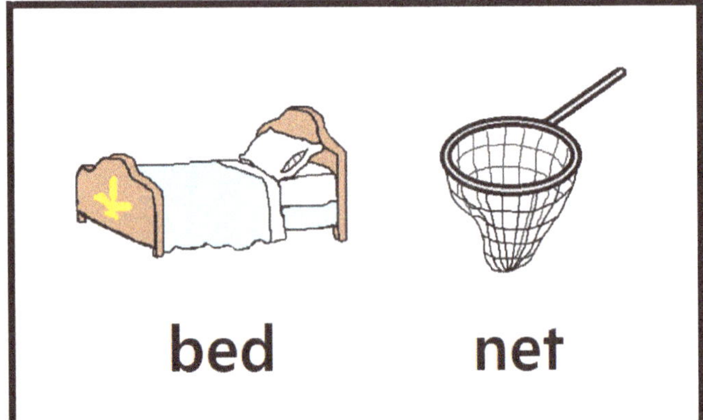

bed   **net**

pig   **win**

cop   **hot**

bus   **sun**

Exercises

Listen and write the last two letters

Tracks 60-69

1 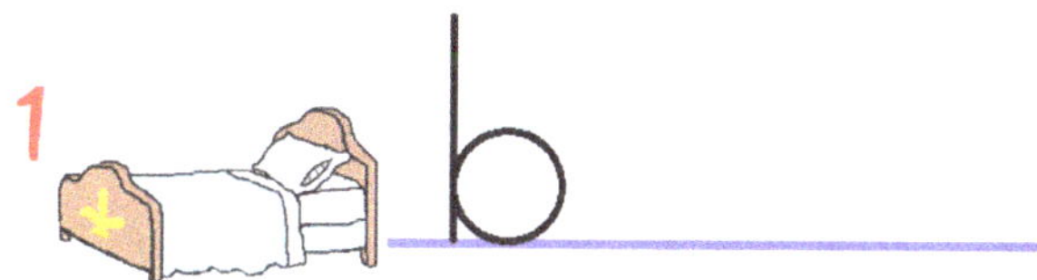 b ______

2 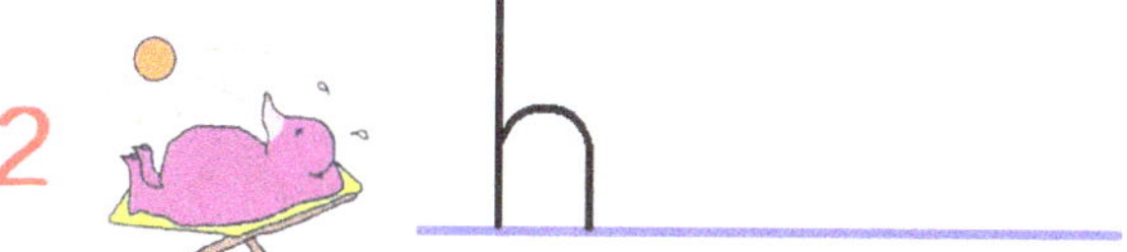 h ______

3 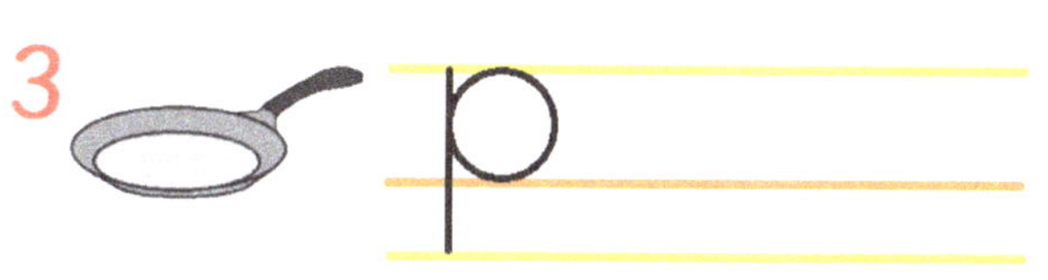 p

4 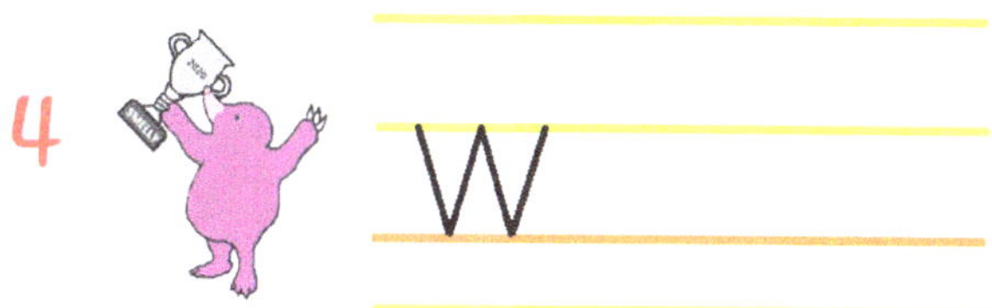 W

Listen and circle the right letters AND picture

1 us un at  

2 op et in  

3 ap un ig  

4 an et ad 

5 ap ig ed 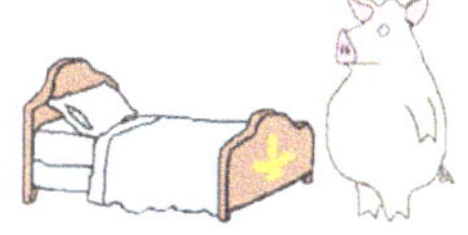

6 ot ag op 

Exercises

Circle the word you hear

Tracks 60-69

Write the word to match the picture

____

Chant

New sight words: call

Hot pig on a bus

Get the net

Call a cop!

Call a cop!

Get the net

Circle the last two letters of the word you hear

Tracks 60-69

1. us   et   un   2. ed   in   ap

3. ap   ig   op   4. an   ed   ot

Listen and read along

New sight words: must   need

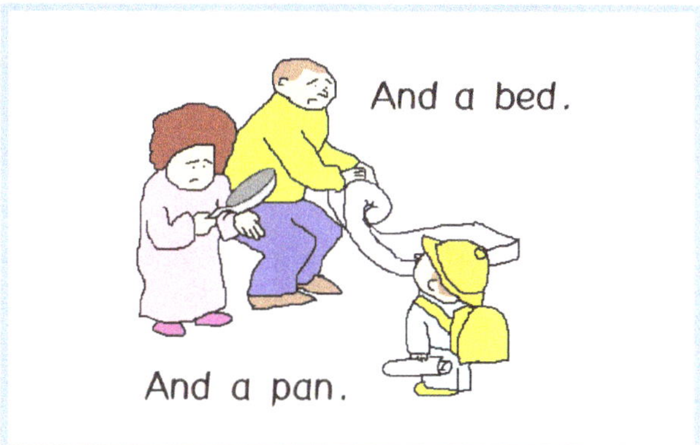

Review

Listen and repeat all the words

1

ob

og

on

2

op

ot

ox

3

ub

ud

ug

4

un

up

ut

5

ap
an
ed
et
ig

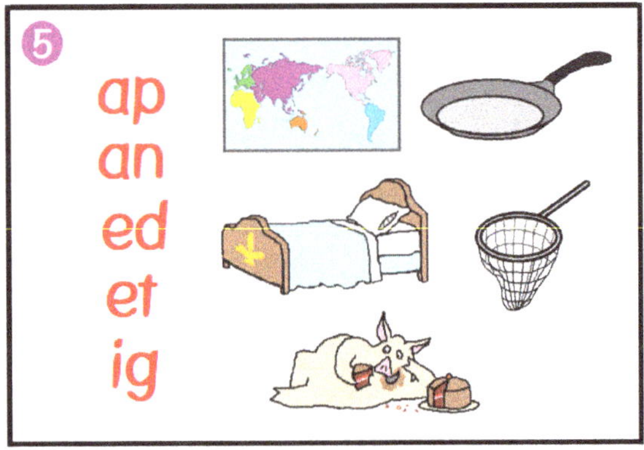

6

in
op
ot
us
un

Review

1  ___________________

2 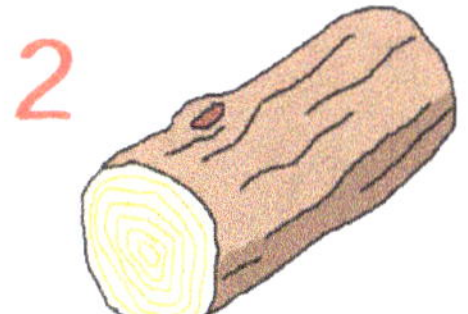 ___________________

3 

4 

5  ___________________

6 ___________________

Review

Find the path

a						**a**
e						**e**
i						**i**
o			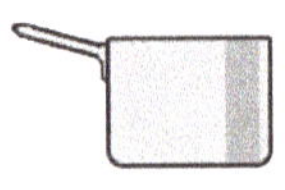	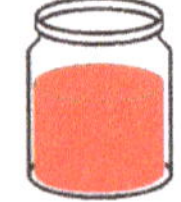		**o**
u		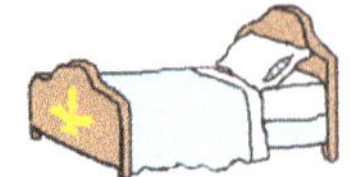		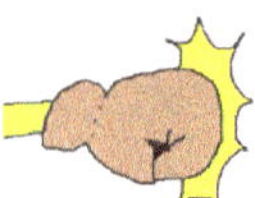		**u**

Listen to the final sound and circle the right word

Tracks 60-69

1   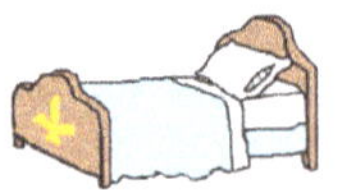

2   

3   

4   

Review

Listen and circle. Then write the word.

Tracks 60-69

1

____

2

____

3
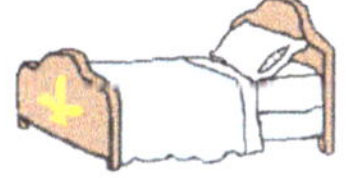

____

4

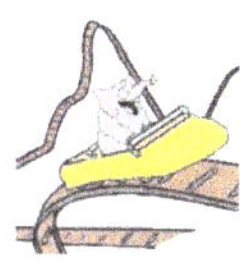
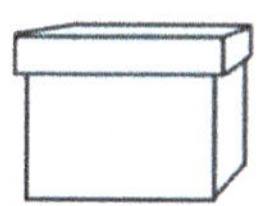

____

5

____

Test

Listen and circle the word you hear

a  Track 69 b 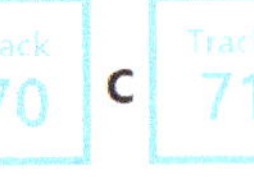 Track 70 c Track 71

1      

2      

3 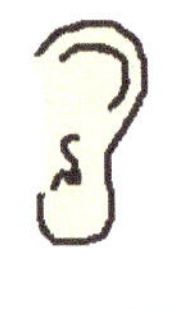     

4      

5   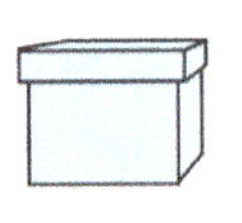 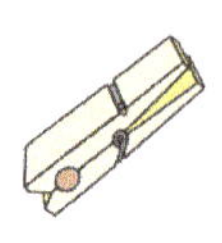  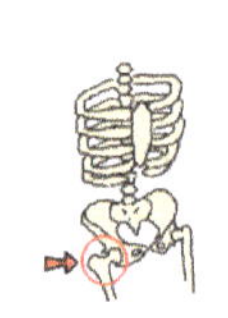

Listen and write the middle letter a  Track 72 b Track 73 c Track 74 

Tracks 70-78

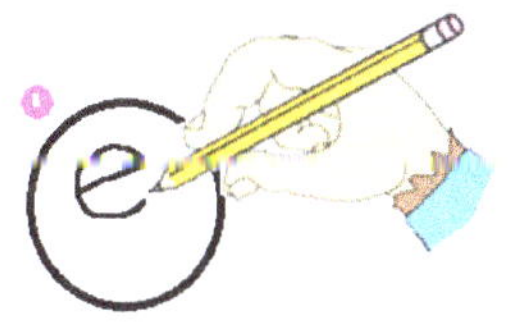

1 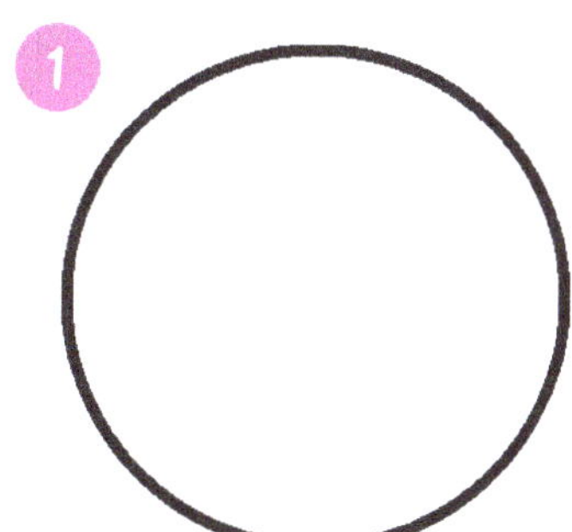

2 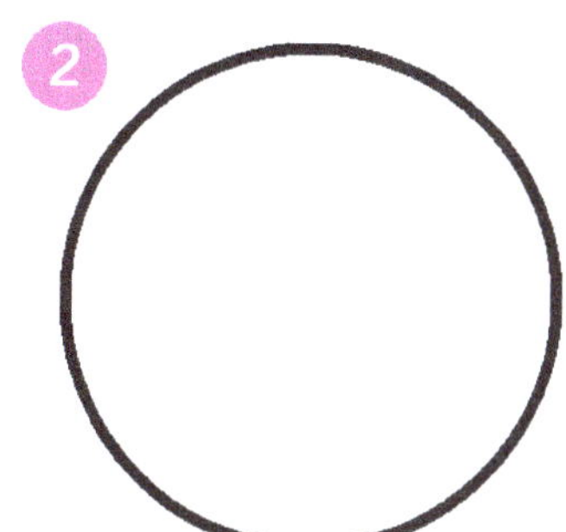

3 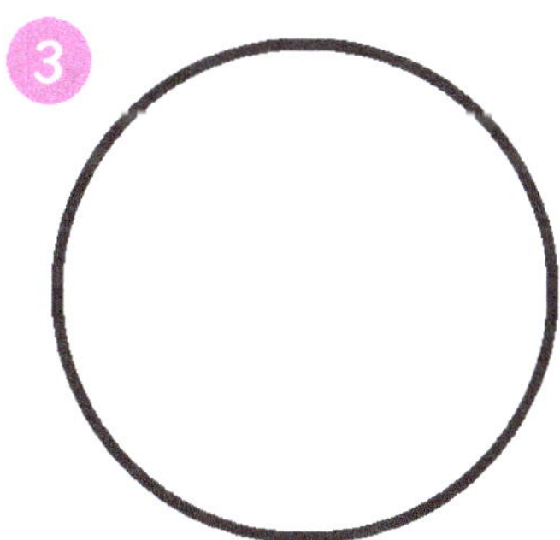

4 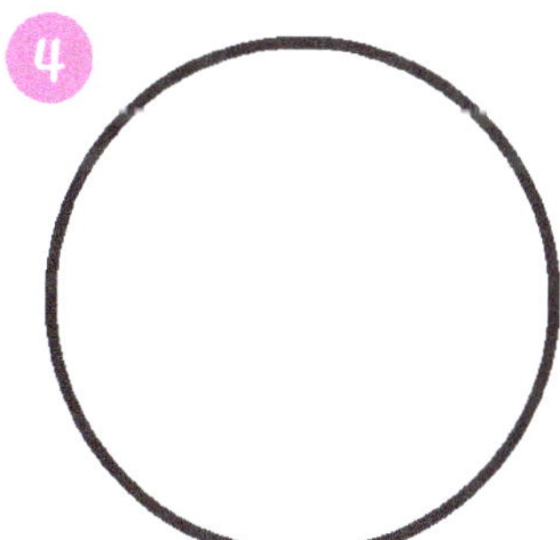

5 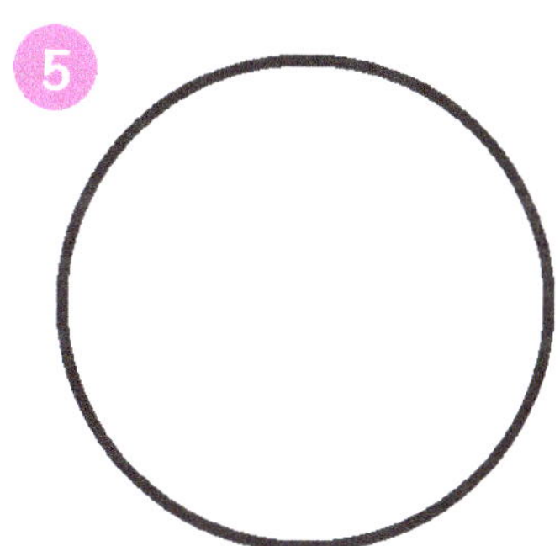

6 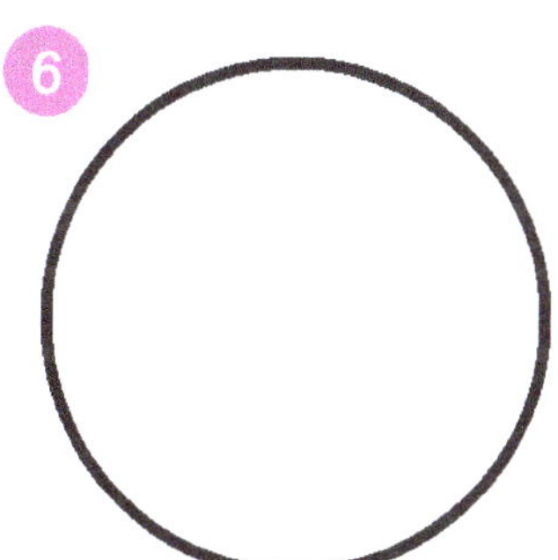

Test

Listen and circle the last two letters a b c

Tracks 70-78

1  at | en | it | op | ut

2  ad | et | in | ob | un

3  ag | ed | id | og | up

4  an | eg | ip | ot | ub

5  am | ell | ig | on | ud

Write the word to match the picture

Tracks 70-78

1 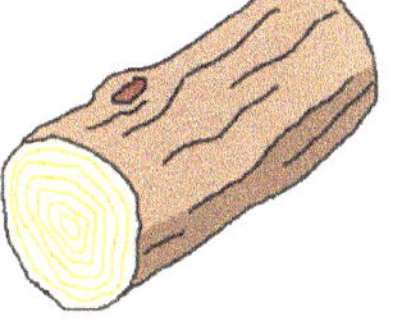 _______________

2  _______________

3 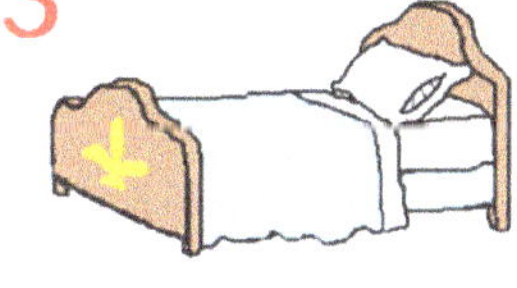 _______________

4  _______________

5  _______________

6 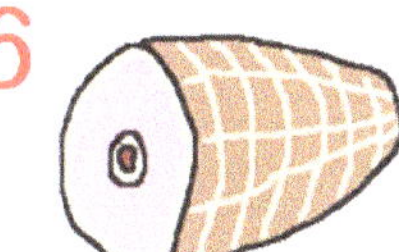 _______________

This is the end
of the book!

Word List

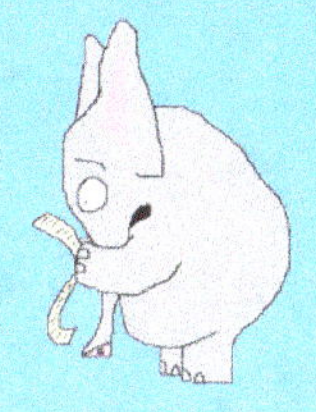

Unit 1

bad

dad

bag

nag

ham

jam

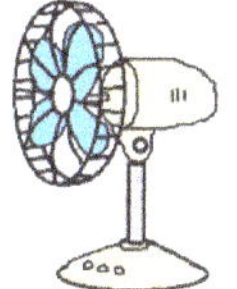

fan

man

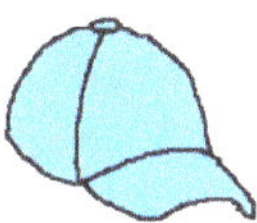

cap

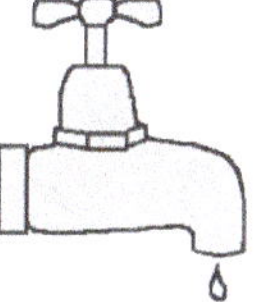

tap

fat

rat

Unit 2

Deb

web

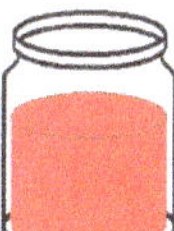

red

wed

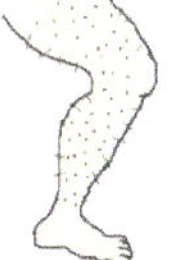

leg

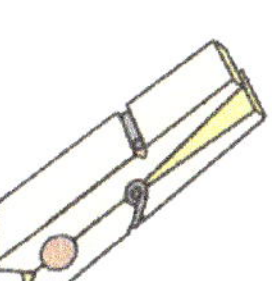

peg

bell

well

men

pen

pet

wet

Word List

Unit 3

bib

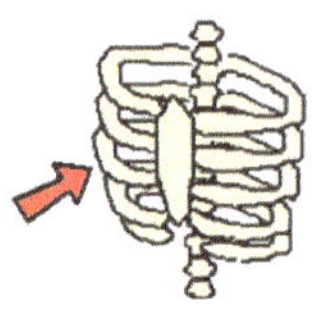
rib

kid

lid

big

wig

bin

fin

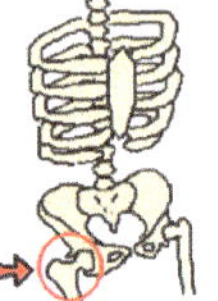
hip

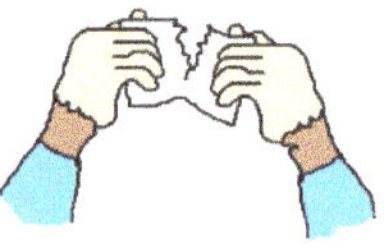
rip

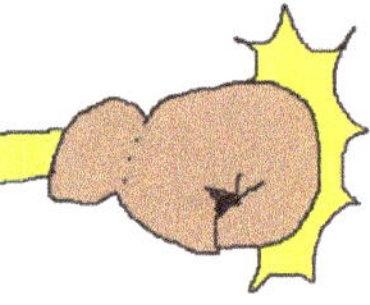
hit

sit

Unit 4

rob

sob

dog

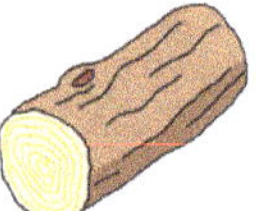
log

on

Ron

hop

mop

got

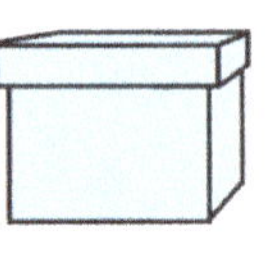
pot

box

fox

Word List

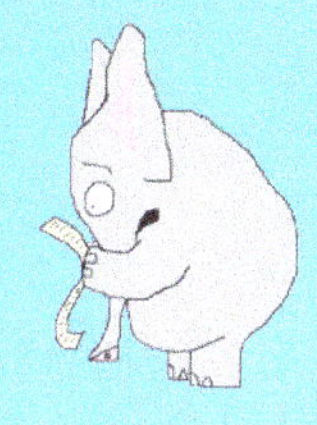

Unit 5

sub

tub

bud

mud

bug

hug

fun

run

cup

pup

cut

hut

Unit 6

map

pan

bed

net

pig

win

cop

hot

bus

sun

Phonics Series

Preschool:

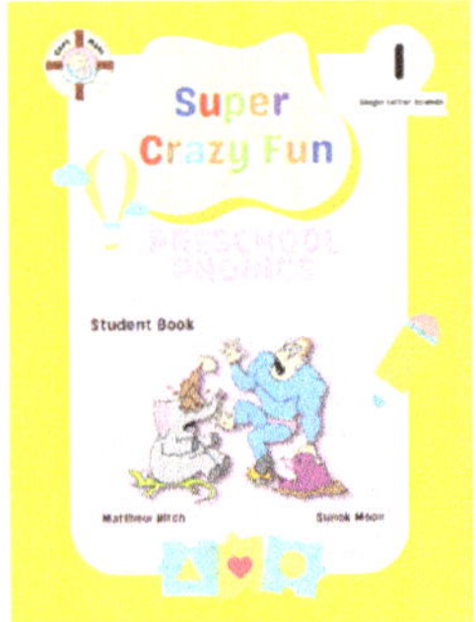 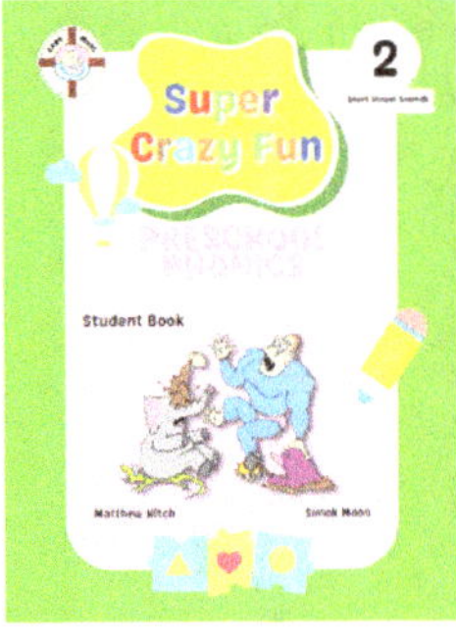   

Kindergarten:

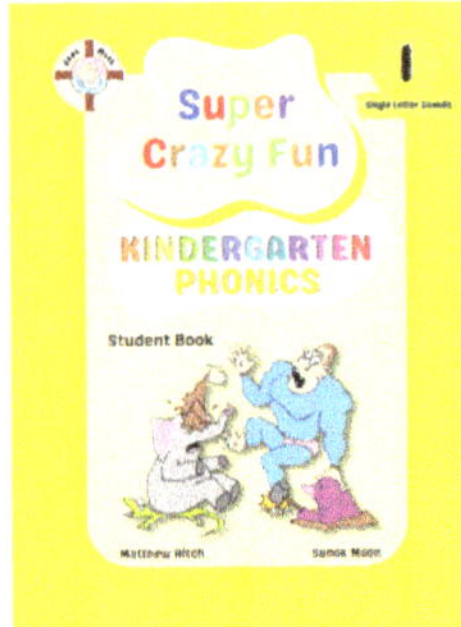 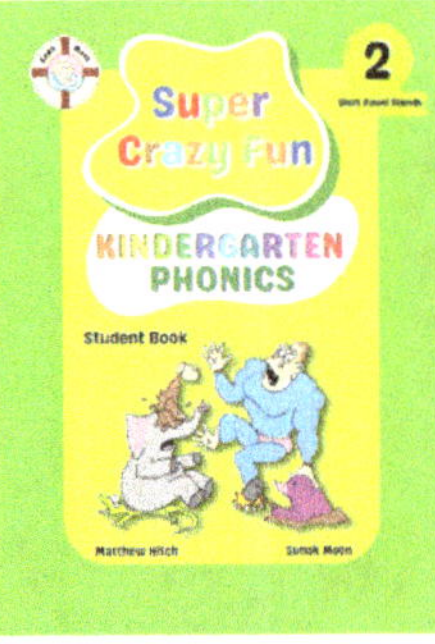   

Elementary School Junior:

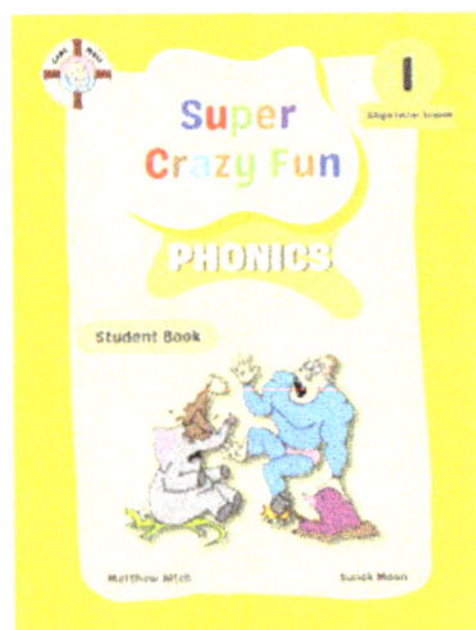 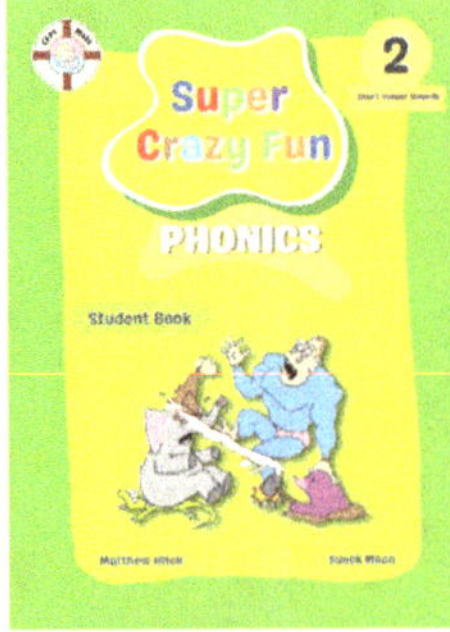   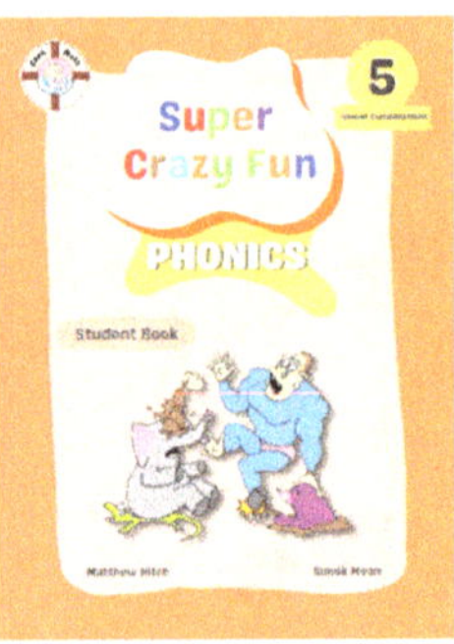

Elementary School Senior/Remedial:

 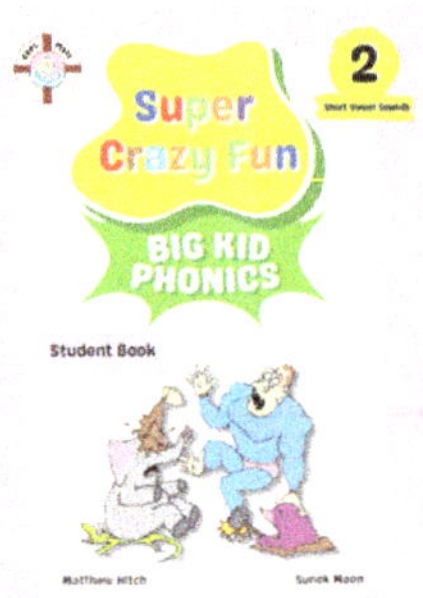 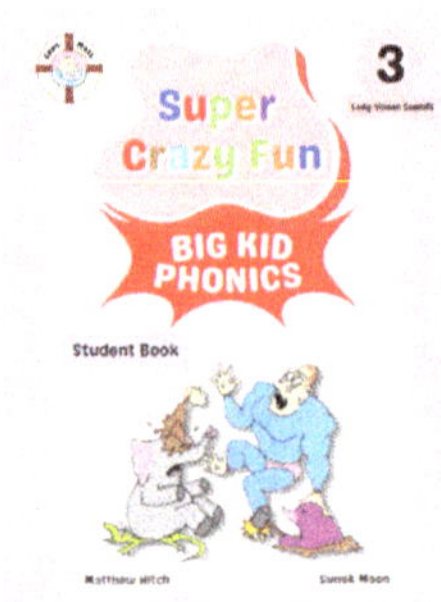  

OUR SIGHT WORD FLASH CARDS!

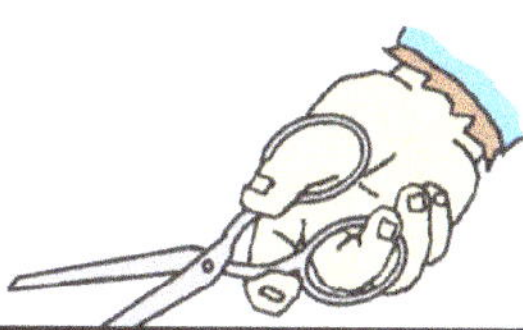

my	am
she	wear
so	will

OUR SIGHT WORD FLASH CARDS!

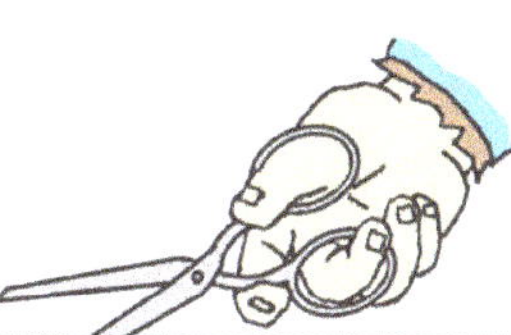

want

give

me

have

he

handsome

OUR SIGHT WORD FLASH CARDS!

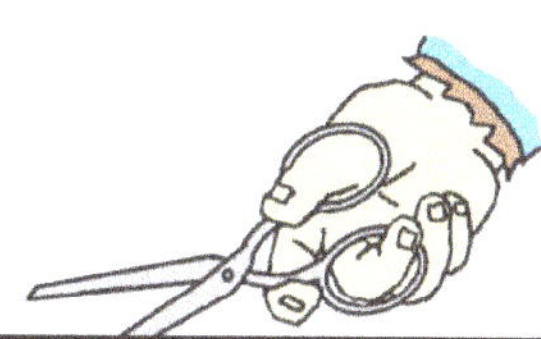

pretty

let's

what

cent

see

call

OUR SIGHT WORD FLASH CARDS!

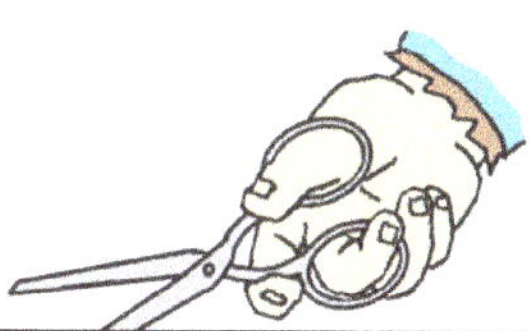

must

need

a / an

and

all

on

OUR SIGHT WORD FLASH CARDS!

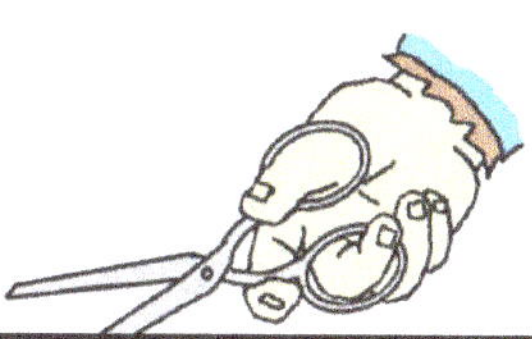

in

the

no

lift

like

get

OUR SIGHT WORD FLASH CARDS!

oh

not

did

you

your

has

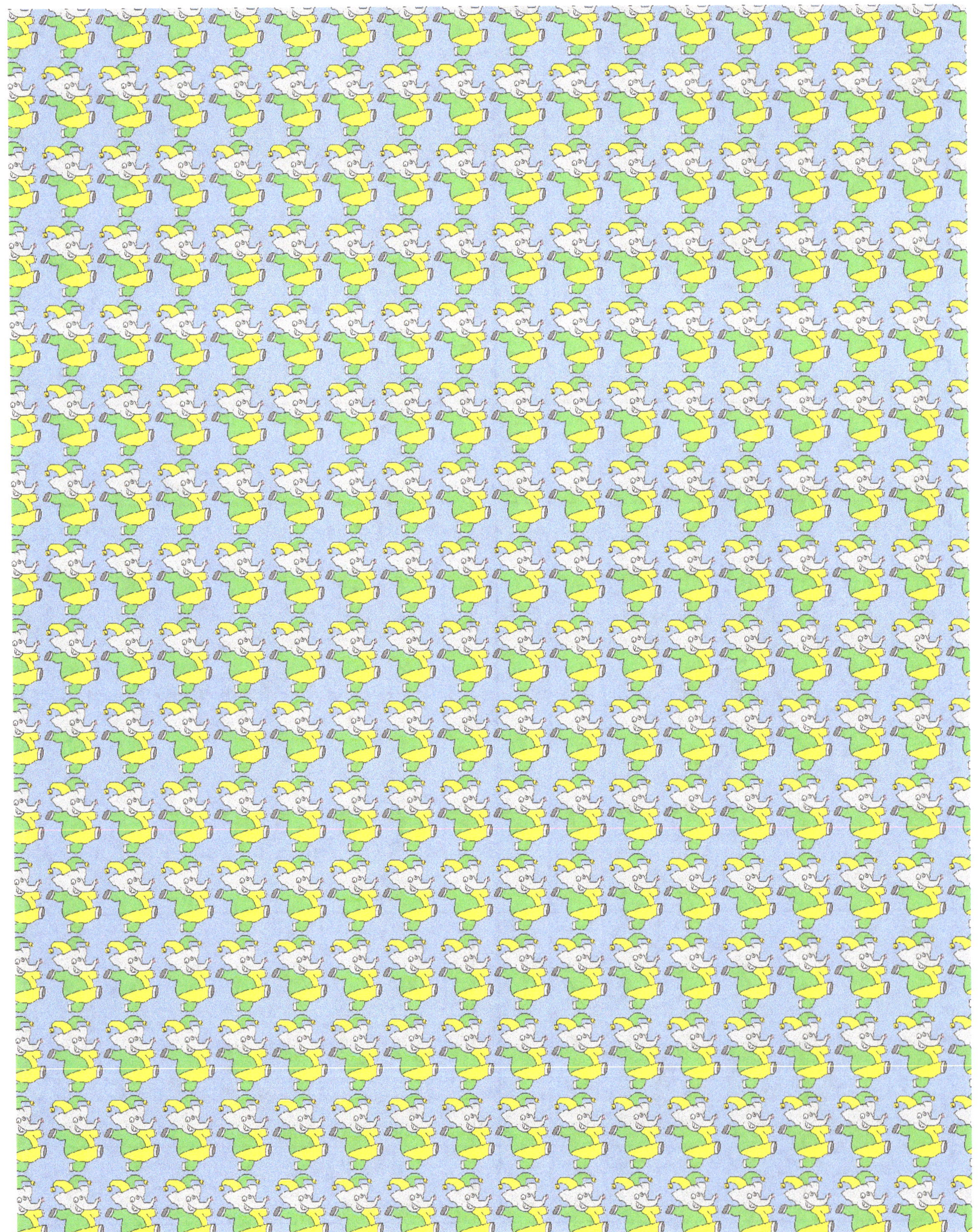

OUR SIGHT WORD FLASH CARDS!

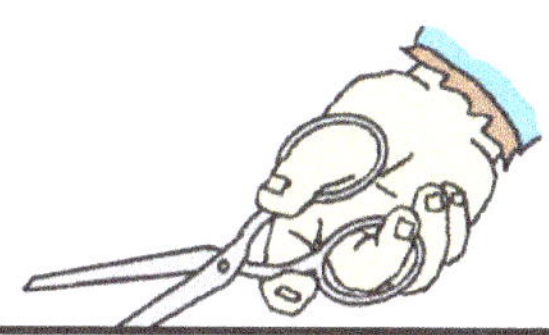

put

one

by

say

go

to

OUR SIGHT WORD FLASH CARDS!

win

had

it

wait

Coloring Pages!!

A

NAG

Coloring Pages!!

E

DEB

Coloring Pages!!

I

BIG

Coloring Pages!!

O

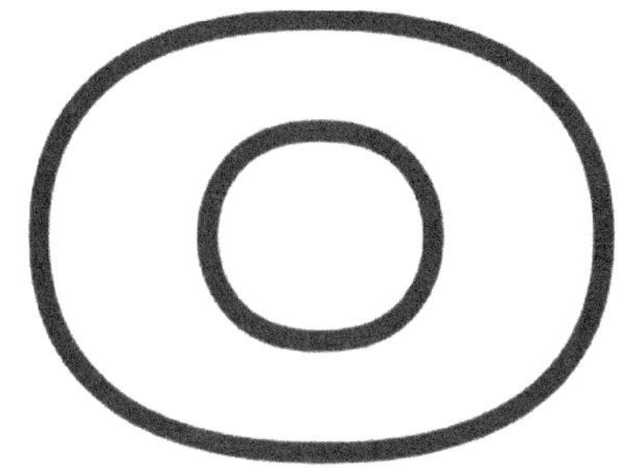

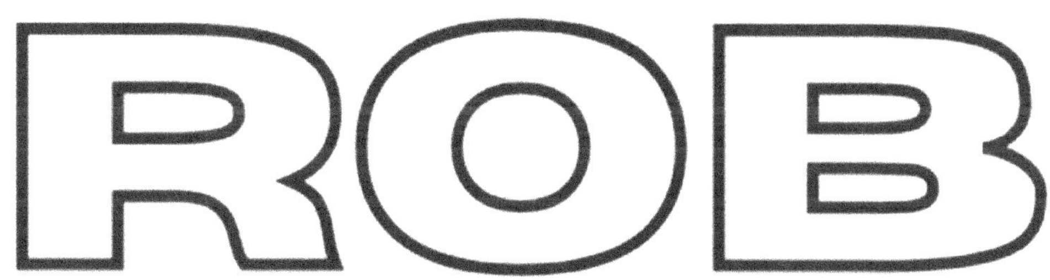

ROB

Coloring Pages!!

U

HUG

Phonics Series

Preschool:

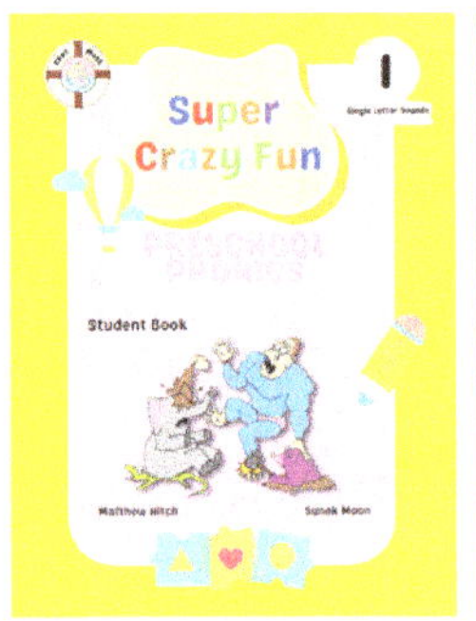 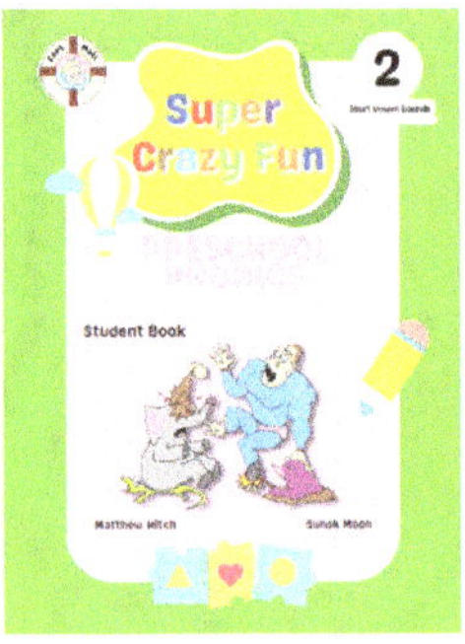   

Kindergarten:

Elementary School Junior:

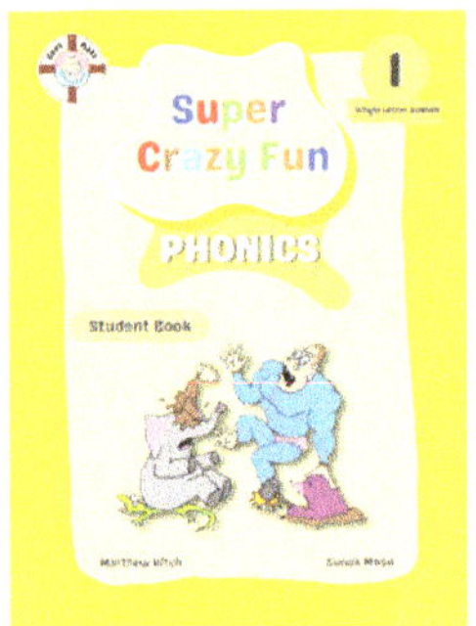 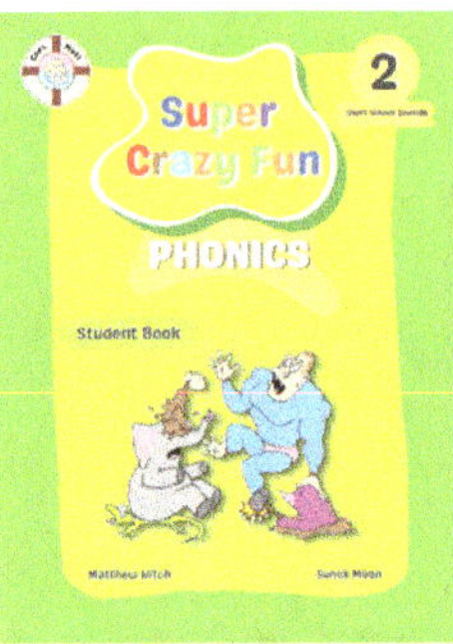   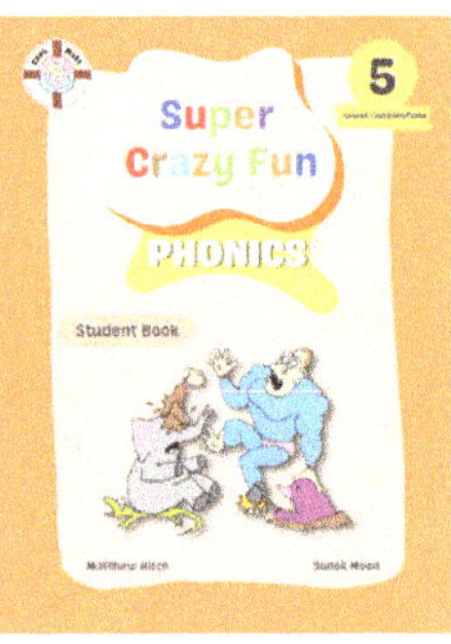

Elementary School Senior/Remedial:

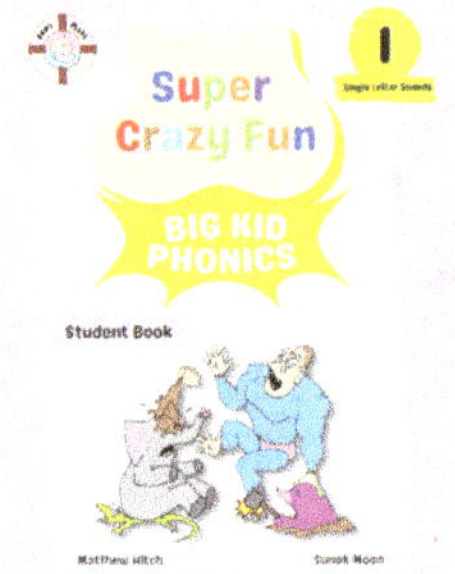  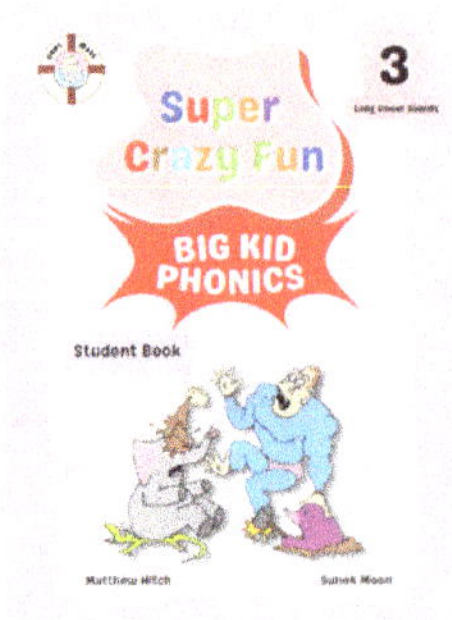 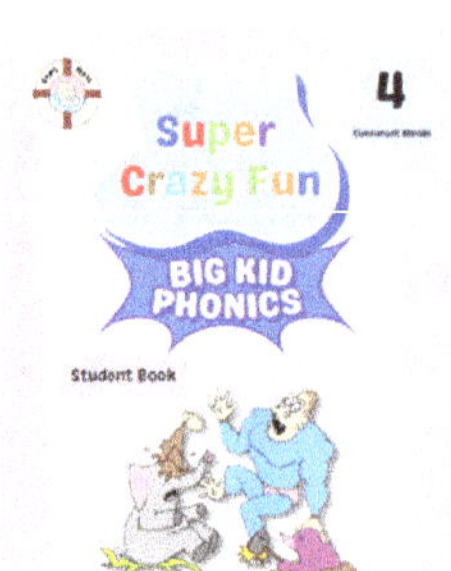 

25 103 210	0 102 255	0 91 158	63 72 204	0 0 204	0 0 255	68 134 255	0 72 204	14 49 190	0 72 204	14 49 190	57 53 238	20 16 188	0 0 222	22 92 188	219 36 60
62 2 202	104 40 253	99 31 226	91 6 176	131 68 176	255 0 255	173 68 200	199 69 196	255 128 255	255 0 255	255 128 192	255 108 156	255 83 169	245 114 153	235 95 175	240 117 197
255 0 0	255 0 19	222 33 52	237 18 95	219 36 60	238 32 94	242 60 6	237 81 35	254 96 1	255 115 0	243 125 29	252 149 46	255 145 77	253 181 83	255 255 123	244 225 89
251 238 0 *	240 228 11	255 255 0	255 247 91	239 250 44	228 241 65	194 235 71	151 228 35	53 217 102	90 186 74	20 224 158	3 241 211	3 134 190	66 99 191	12 81 243	27 82 226